Colombo Commission

Report to the Council of Europe

Strasbourg
June 1986

Report of the Colombo Commission.
French Edition: ISBN 92-871-0888-9
German Edition: ISBN 92-871-0892-7
Italian Edition: ISBN 92-871-0894-3

Colombo Commission. Appendix to the report. Complementary explanatory notes.
French Edition: ISBN 92-871-0889-7
English Edition: ISBN 92-871-0891-9
German Edition: ISBN 92-871-0893-5
Italian Edition: ISBN 92-871-0895-1

Strasbourg, Council of Europe, Publications Section, 1986
ISBN 92-871-0890-0
Printed in the Federal Republic of Germany

MEMBERSHIP OF THE COMMISSION

Mr Emilio Colombo (Italy), *Chairman*, member of the Italian parliament, former Prime Minister, former Minister for Foreign Affairs, former President of the European Parliament, winner of the Charlemagne Prize (Christian Democrat)

Mrs Hélène Ahrweiler (France), Rector of the Paris Education Authority, Chancellor of the Paris Universities, Secretary General of the International Committee for Historical Science

Mr José-Maria de Areilza (Spain), former Minister for Foreign Affairs, former President of the Parliamentary Assembly of the Council of Europe (Independent Liberal)

Mr Pieter Dankert (Netherlands), member and former President of the European Parliament, former member of the Parliamentary Assembly of the Council of Europe (Socialist)

Mr Maurice Faure (France), Senator, former minister, former member of the European Parliament (Movement of the Radical Left)

Mr Knut Frydenlund (Norway), Minister for Foreign Affairs, former member of the Parliamentary Assembly of the Council of Europe (Socialist)

Mr Kai Uwe von Hassel (Federal Republic of Germany), former minister, former member of the European Parliament, former President of the *Bundestag* and of the Assembly of Western European Union (Christian Democrat)

Mr Alois Mock (Austria), Chairman of the International Democratic Union, *Nationalrat* (Christian Democrat)

Mr Geoffrey Rippon (United Kingdom), MP, former Chancellor of the Duchy of Lancaster, former member of the European Parliament and of the Parliamentary Assembly of the Council of Europe (Conservative)

Notes:

1. Mr Ludwig Steiner (Austria), former State Secretary for Foreign Affairs, former Ambassador, Vice-President of the European Christian Democratic Union, member of the Parliamentary Assembly of the Council of Europe (Christian Democrat) deputised for Mr Mock at some of the Commission's meetings.

2. Mr Heinrich Klebes, Mr Jean-Louis Laurens and Mr Giovanni Palmieri acted as Secretaries to the Commission.

CONTENTS

	Page
Report to the Council of Europe.	11
Political affairs	14
— Political dialogue	14
— A European democratic area	15
— The Council of Europe and the Community	16
— Relations with the other Europe	17
Human rights	19
— Safeguarding human rights	19
— Citizens' rights	20
— Parliamentary democracy	21
— Problems of present-day society	21
— Family problems and equality between the sexes	22
Culture	24
— Cultural identity	24
— Education and training of the young	25
Research, science and technology	27
Harmonisation of law	28
Regional and local authorities	29
Means of co-operation	30
Conclusion	31

FOREWORD

The Colombo Commission (Commission of eminent European personalities) was set up, in accordance with Recommendation 994 adopted by the Parliamentary Assembly of the Council of Europe on 3 October 1984. In the appendix to that recommendation the Commission was instructed to work out future perspectives for European co-operation beyond the present decade.

The members of the Commission serve in their individual capacities, independently of their national or international affiliations. Bearing in mind, *inter alia*, the parallel work of the *ad hoc* committees set up by the European Council at Fontainebleau in June 1984,[1] the Commission has instructions:

— to "present views and proposals conducive to strengthening the co-operation between all the democratic states of Europe in order to avoid a widening gap between them";

— to "present bold and realistic suggestions, encompassing the main areas of the lives of European nationals, that might contribute towards the creation of a fully united Europe";

— to "look into the adequacy of existing European institutions with a view to the realities and requirements of the Europe of tomorrow";

— to "present long-term proposals as well as proposals which lend themselves to immediate follow-up and implementation at a practical level, for the benefit of the European citizen".

While its mandate requires the Commission to keep in mind the broader perspective of Europe, encompassing more than the Western European democracies, it emphasises that its primary task should be to strengthen the unity of the pluralistic democracies of Europe and to counter tendencies away from such unity.

---

1. Institutional Committee chaired by Mr Dooge and Citizens' Europe Committee chaired by Mr Adonnino.

The Commission submitted a first interim report (included in this report) to the President of the Assembly, the Chairman of the Committee of Ministers and the Secretary General of the Council of Europe on 12 June 1985.

Since that date, a number of important events have taken place on the European stage, such as the Milan Summit, at which it was decided to convene an intergovernmental conference to revise the European treaties and at which the proposals of the Adonnino report on a People's Europe were endorsed; the Bremen Conference, which launched the Eureka project, now involving eighteen European states; the intergovernmental conference itself, followed by the Luxembourg Summit, which led to the adoption of the Single European Act; and lastly, on 1 January 1986, the accession of two more member states to the European Community. Within the Council of Europe, the same period was marked by the negotiations initiated by the Secretary General with the Community institutions, with a view to strengthening co-operation between the Twelve and the Twenty-one at both institutional and operational level as well as by the publication of the draft Third Medium-Term Plan, 1987–1991, entitled "Democratic Europe: humanism, diversity, universality". A further feature of the period was the examination of and follow-up to the Colombo Commission's first report.

In its Recommendation 1017, the Assembly, whilst supporting the Commission's proposals as a whole, singled out certain proposals which it hoped to see implemented as a matter of urgency. Recommendation 1017 was the basis for the exchange of views between the Committee of Ministers and the Assembly during the Joint Committee on 20 November 1985. In that same recommendation, the Assembly expressed the wish that the Commission should deal, *inter alia*, with "the compatibility between the Adonnino proposals on a People's Europe and those of the first Colombo report, and with possibilities of European co-operation across the frontiers between the different economic and political systems". The Assembly also invited the Commission to look into family problems.

These wishes largely coincide with the intentions of the Commission itself, which concluded its interim report with a proposal to complete its mandate by going further into certain questions dealt with therein and making "proposals of direct concern to the lives of citizens, progress with the building of Europe and the contributions of the different institutions". It also announced its intention of examining "the scope for European co-operation across the frontiers dividing the continent's economic and political systems".

It was with these objectives in mind and in the light of the major developments in Europe in recent months that the Commission embarked on the second phase of its work, which led to the present report, in which the Commission completes the mandate given to it by the Parliamentary Assembly.

REPORT TO THE COUNCIL OF EUROPE

Europe in the widest sense, with some thirty independent sovereign states, is no mere geographical concept. Every European has the feeling of bearing the stamp of a common civilisation and culture, expressive of an unconditional attachment to humanist values based on respect for the individual and his rights. Whilst it is the product of forms specific to various European peoples, the European spirit is to be regarded as a unity based on humanism in all its aspects and however expressed. It is in this unity that men and women of all European countries aspire to live, regardless of political frontiers. The differences and barriers that have stood in the way of unity and peace in Europe down through history have been powerless to eradicate this feeling.

Today the division of Europe resulting from the second world war considerably restricts possibilities of pan-European co-operation. But the European states based on parliamentary democracy and respect for human rights constitute a homogeneous whole. They bear witness to Europe's striving after democracy, freedom, justice and the rule of law. It is essential to affirm their political identity on the international scene. The co-operation between them is of a very special kind, differing from traditional international co-operation. Whereas the latter is based on the concept of interdependence, the former is also induced by democratic solidarity.

Inside democratic Europe several international institutions are at work, but two are playing a preponderant role: the Council of Europe and the European Community. While their methods and resources differ, both were created in response to the same need; both were borne along in the early post-war years by the momentum of a strong aspiration for unity between states and between peoples in Europe and for a new type of European international relations, one designed to preserve peace, democracy and human rights and to foster economic and social development.

The Council of Europe was conceived as an instrument for achieving unity through co-operation. Today, it constitutes the largest framework for participation by the states of democratic Europe as well as for co-operation between these states in matters within its sphere of competence. It is also the framework which underlines most effectively the permanent political value of our continent's fundamental cultural unity, despite its division, a unity which the younger generations must rediscover, gradually and peacefully.

The European Community was established for the purpose of bringing about integration in clearly defined areas, thus acting as a springboard for integration in other areas. It uses the means of action prescribed by the treaties in order to give flesh and blood to the idea which prompted its establishment and has guided its development: the formation of a European union. It has acquired an economic personality which prefigures the forms future political unity will take. The Community, whose powers have been widened gradually over the years, has recently extended its boundaries to encompass Spain and Portugal. In adopting the Single European Act, it has just taken another step forward on the road to European unity. All who support the idea of European unity must welcome this, for it is the central dynamic element in the process of European unification. However, the geographical enlargement of the Community and the progressive development of its powers must be accompanied by a reinforcement of co-operation among the Twenty-one. That is to say, the very grave risk, for the family of European democratic states, of a widening of the gap already existing between members of the Community and the other members of the Council of Europe must be avoided. In this context the Council's political role of reaffirming our continent's highest democratic and cultural values is a permanent safeguard.

Accordingly, it is important that the governments of the Twenty-one should do their utmost to develop cohesion among all the European states dedicated to an idea of society based on the common values of democracy, the rule of law, respect for the rights of the individual, social justice and quality of life.

Confronted with this Community dynamic (geographical enlargement and increased powers), the Council of Europe should concentrate on two areas:

i. involving all the democratic European countries in the progress of European unification. The Commission's whole thinking is guided by the principle that every effort must be made to avoid dividing Europe by neglecting the countries which are not members of the Community;

ii. developing European co-operation among the Twenty-one. This co-operation prepares the ground for the Community's more ambitious and binding action. There are spheres and problems which do not lend themselves directly to Community integration but can be made the subject of more flexible co-operation. Co-operation makes it possible to harmonise national approaches and policies to some extent; it thus paves the way for a more unitary approach, that of integration.

It is with these two approaches in mind that the Commission presents the following recommendations.

POLITICAL AFFAIRS

Political dialogue

The Commission considers that the Council of Europe, by reason of its membership and the political character conferred on it by its Statute, should develop and intensify political dialogue among its member states. This dialogue should strengthen the links between the Community's "European Political Co-operation"[1] and the other members of the Council of Europe and thus increase Europe's weight on the world scene. The Commission consequently recommends:

a. an intensification of political dialogue in the Council of Europe at different levels, more particularly at ministerial level, the following being priority themes:

— harmonisation of the positions and activities of member states on major issues of international politics;

— East-West relations, with particular reference to the CSCE process;

— relations between democratic Europe and the world's other democracies;

— problems which arise in bilateral relations between member states;

b. an exchange of views between the member states of the Council of Europe and the Community to co-ordinate their positions in wider international forums;

c. presentation to the Parliamentary Assembly of the Council of Europe, by procedures to be mutually agreed, of the conclusions of political dialogue between governments, with a view to taking advantage

---

1. As decided in general principle by the Conference of Heads of State or Government of the member states of the European Community, meeting in The Hague on 2 December 1969, and whose objectives were defined in greater detail in the first report by the Ministers for Foreign Affairs to the Heads of State or Government, dated 27 October 1970 (Luxembourg Report).

of the Assembly's deliberative and stimulating function in the political sphere.

The political aspects of the building of Europe should be examined in depth in political dialogue between governments and in parliamentary political debate, with all Council of Europe member states taking part in discussions on Europe's future. The Parliamentary Assembly could hold general debates at regular intervals on the progress of European construction, based on reports from the Secretary General and with participation by the Committee of Ministers. National delegations should ensure that this debate is continued in national parliaments.[1]

A European democratic area

Europe is a diverse reality embodied in a large number of organisations comprising varying numbers of European states. One of these, the European Community, favours integration as the way ahead; the others give priority to co-operation. Of the latter, some play a specialised role (in economic, military, cultural, scientific or technical matters); others, including the Council of Europe, play a general role. This diversity among the organisations in their composition, ways of operating and aims, reflects both the different levels of each state's European commitment, and the existence of different forms of solidarity that complement one another. The Council of Europe is the forum giving broadest expression to the essential solidarity among democratic European states attached to fundamental freedoms and human rights.

The Commission observes that any form of European co-operation requires a minimum amount of cohesion and solidarity among the participant states. In its view, this is attested by the weakness of pan-European co-operation. It considers that promoting such cohesion and solidarity among the European parliamentary democracies is the daily task of the Council of Europe and its chief contribution to European unification. The Europe of democracy and human rights provides an area in which other initiatives of a bolder kind can flourish. The Commission considers that the links between the Council of Europe and the other European institutions are inadequate. The various organisations' efforts are often dissipated, which impairs their effectiveness and their impact on the European public.

---

1. This proposal already featured in the interim report. An initial debate on the progress of European construction along the lines proposed by the Commission was held during the Assembly's April 1986 part-session.

Accordingly, the Commission recommends:

i. establishing closer working relations between all the organisations active in Europe, to avoid duplication of work and also to mobilise all available resources and skills;

ii. maintaining and reinforcing the role of the Parliamentary Assembly as a discussion forum for those European organisations with no parliamentary organ of their own. In that context, the Parliamentary Assembly, which already holds regular debates on the activities of OECD, EFTA and the European Conference of Ministers of Transport, should undertake to perform a similar function for the activities of other organisations, in particular Eureka;

iii. ensuring compatibility in the work of the different organisations, particularly in the norms and rules they prescribe, and better co-ordination of their present and future programmes of activities. To that end, it hopes that regular information exchanges will take place between the departments responsible for programming and planning in each organisation.

The Council of Europe and the Community

The Commission is convinced that the European Community should become a full participant in multilateral co-operation within the Council of Europe. To that end it recommends in particular:

a. Strengthening the links between the European Community and the Council of Europe in the spirit of the mandate given to the Secretary General by the Council of Europe's Committee of Ministers (Resolution (85) 5 of 25 April 1985);

b. Convening informal meetings of the specialist ministers of the Twenty-one in liaison with the Community's Council of Ministers to consider possible ways of extending European co-operation;

c. Intensifying relations between the parliamentary assemblies of the two institutions, in order to enable each of them to deliberate in full knowledge of the other's activities in both the political and the technical spheres;

d. Establishing regular contacts between:

i. the Chairman of the Council of Europe's Committee of Ministers and the President of the Council of Ministers of the Community (either the President of the "general" Council made up of the Ministers for Foreign Affairs, or, depending on the questions to be dealt with, the President of one or other of the specialised councils);

ii. the chairmen and rapporteurs of those committees of the Parliamentary Assembly of the Council of Europe and the European Parliament dealing with similar matters. Such contacts would complement the meetings that already take place between the Presidents and delegations from the Bureaux of the two assemblies, which should be held more frequently;

iii. the Secretary General of the Council of Europe and the President of the Commission of the European Communities. These contacts should be extended by a regular flow of information between the Council of Europe Secretariat and the departments of the Commission. In that context, the Commission recommends the setting up of a system of staff exchanges and secondments between the two institutions.

The Commission welcomes the decision by the European Council to follow the recommendations of the Adonnino report that the European flag and European anthem should be those already used by the Council of Europe; it hopes that a satisfactory solution may be found to the question of celebrating Europe Day on the same date throughout Europe.

The Commission considers that accession by the Community to the Council of Europe's legal instruments will be simplified if the Community is involved in their drafting. For that purpose, the Community should be granted a general right to participate in the meetings of Council of Europe committees of experts. For its part, the Council of Europe should be present, under arrangements to be negotiated, at meetings of experts drafting Community regulations and directives that may subsequently be extended to non-Community states.

Lastly, the Commission considers that an essential step forward in European co-operation would be taken through the participation by the Community as such in Council of Europe activities, in ways to be defined in the spirit of Article 230 of the Treaty of Rome: this might go as far as accession to the Statute of the Council of Europe.

Relations with the other Europe

The Commission considers that dialogue in the cultural field is of paramount importance in maintaining, developing and deepening the links which transcend the present division of our continent.

Establishment of lasting peace in Europe requires continuous political dialogue as well as bilateral and multilateral co-operation between all European states. By virtue of its composition and the nature of its activities, the Council of Europe is well qualified to be the instrument of European co-operation across the frontier dividing two economic and political systems. It therefore lies with the Council to seek contacts and co-operation with the non-member European countries in fields within its competence which concern Europe as a whole. The cohesion between Council of Europe member states is founded on shared values (parliamentary democracy, the rule of law, respect for human rights). Accordingly, dialogue and co-operation with the other Europe must take place with due respect for those principles. Any dialogue or co-operation presupposes a political will on both sides.

Consequently, the Commission recommends:

a. that the non-member European states be informed of the Council of Europe's readiness to engage in dialogue and co-operate not only in the sphere of culture but also in other fields within its competence such as education, sport, youth, health, the environment and drug dependence;

b. that the Secretary General of the Council of Europe be instructed to approach the governments of these states with a view to determining the fields in which co-operation might be envisaged and working out the practical arrangements;

c. that contacts be established at parliamentary level between the Parliamentary Assembly and the non-member European countries, in particular in the fields of culture, the environment and transfrontier co-operation;

d. that the Committee of Ministers, in the framework of its political dialogue, actively prepare the participation of member states in all the CSCE meetings and conferences, so that they may present joint positions and proposals;

e. that the Parliamentary Assembly hold round tables on various aspects of the CSCE, with participants from non-member states.

HUMAN RIGHTS

Safeguarding human rights

The Commission points out that the commitment of member states of the Council of Europe to human rights entails a continuous adaptation of the system of protection instituted by the Convention for the Protection of Human Rights and Fundamental Freedoms (hereafter referred to as "the convention") to the imperatives of everyday life and the evolution of society, as manifested for example in the problems raised by scientific and technical progress in such matters as data protection, biotechnology and the growth of the media.

The Commission appeals to all states parties to the convention which have not yet done so to accept the optional clauses embodied in Articles 25 (right of individual petition) and 46 (jurisdiction of the Court) of the convention. It also appeals to all states parties to the convention to sign and ratify the protocols to the convention and to incorporate all these instruments into their domestic law.

The Commission further recommends:

a. a review of the procedural aspects of the machinery for the protection of human rights instituted by the convention, over and above the provisions of Protocol No. 8, to enable the organs of the convention to discharge their duties with maximum efficiency;

b. recognition of the right of the individual to refer to the Court applications declared admissible;

c. examination of the desirability of instituting within the Council of Europe, side-by-side with the procedures laid down in the convention, a non-judicial procedure to foster respect for human rights;

d. the study of ways and means to prevent the emergence of two different bodies of case-law (that of the European Court of Human Rights and that of the Court of Justice of the European Communities) on the interpretation of the same rights, one such means being accession by the Community to the convention.

Citizens' rights

European unity, the objective of both the Council of Europe and the Community, implies that the citizens of the twenty-one countries should have a sense of participating in the same venture during their lives and everyday experience. If this is to be the case, it is important in particular to remove all obstacles in the way of free movement of persons, freedom of establishment and freedom to provide services. Significant progress has been made in this direction by the Community which has recognised the principle that a Community state should treat other Community states' nationals in the same way as its own where their rights and obligations are concerned.

With this in view, the Commission recommends that a greater effort be made to identify those Community rules that might be extended to Council of Europe member states as a whole with a view to bringing the citizens of those countries closer together, particularly in the following fields:

— access to industrial, craft and commercial activities;

— free movement of members of private professions;

— conditions governing the exercise of the various occupations;

— treatment in social security matters.

The Commission expresses the wish that every citizen of a Council of Europe member country will be able to obtain a European passport constituting a recognised identity document.

The Commission has studied with interest the proposals of the Adonnino report. Some of these proposals might usefully be applied in the Council of Europe framework. In particular, the Commission recommends:

— that examination be continued of the possibility of according citizens of member states voting rights and eligibility in local elections subject to a certain period of prior residence in the host country;

— that all citizens of the twenty-one member countries be afforded the same rights as nationals regarding freedom of speech and assembly;

— that member states' citizens residing in another member state be consulted whenever decisions of special importance to them are to be taken.

Parliamentary democracy

Parliamentary democracy and respect for human rights are closely linked and constitute basic conditions for membership of the Council of Europe and of the European Community.

The Commission recommends that the Council of Europe pursue and intensify, at parliamentary and governmental levels, and with the participation of the European Community and the other democracies in the world, initiatives launched in 1983 at the first Strasbourg Conference on Parliamentary Democracy, notably:

— discussion of the functioning of parliamentary democracy in member states in its various aspects;

— the establishment of links of solidarity with parliamentary democracies in other parts of the world;

— activities likely to encourage the development of parliamentary democracy in the states of the Third World.

Problems of present-day society

The Commission believes that, if co-operation in dealing with the major problems of present-day society (terrorism, drug addiction, unemployment, pollution) is to be effective, it must include all Europe's democracies. Such co-operation is warranted in order to safeguard the values on which our societies are founded. It therefore recommends:

a. that the Council of Europe draw up a new convention on the combating of *terrorism*, to which all member states will be able to accede. Such a convention should include provisions to ensure that extradition procedures are accompanied by all the necessary safeguards for objectivity and respect for human rights;

b. that all the democratic European states co-operate more actively in the fight against *drug* trafficking, and in the prevention of drug dependence;

c. that all Council of Europe member states—and, if possible, the Community as such—accede to the European Social Charter, the Convention on the Legal Status of Migrant Workers and the Resettlement Fund for National Refugees and Over-population; and that the Council of Europe give serious thought to working out guidelines for the future development of *social policies* in the face of unemployment, the increase in poverty and the ageing of the population, and to encouraging the integration of *migrant workers* in the receiving countries;

d. that all the member states consult together as a matter of priority on *unemployment,* especially among young people, a major problem in present-day society which could endanger the stability of democratic systems;

e. that, for effective protection of the *environment,* identical standards and rules be applied—one means to this end being the extension of Community standards to all Council of Europe member states—and that action be taken jointly by the European Community and the Council of Europe to make people aware of the international scale of the problem.

Family problems and equality between the sexes

The Commission stresses the importance of the Council of Europe's initiatives on two closely related points: family problems and equality between the sexes.

The Council of Europe deals with problems concerning the family. Article 8 of the European Convention on Human Rights recognises and protects the right to respect for family life. The family, a basic element in the social fabric, is now threatened with disintegration as a result of the pressures that profound social changes are bringing to bear on its members, and which condition our everyday lives. The states of democratic Europe must find ways of enhancing the role of the family, thereby enabling it to continue to play its role as a prime repository of the fundamental values of European civilisation.

The Commission recommends:

— that the Council of Europe set itself the task of co-ordinating efforts to promote the adoption in member states of a series of measures relating to family law, labour law and fiscal law in order to give practical effect to the right of every individual to a full family life;

— that the Council of Europe study ways and means of developing and defining social protection duties that the family will have to undertake, notably for the benefit of the elderly, the disabled and the sick;

— that the principle that any act of violence against women and children is liable to mandatory prosecution be affirmed in national legislation of Council of Europe member states.

The Commission is convinced that complete integration of all citizens into the life of society is a *sine qua non* for real social progress. It is accordingly important that equality between the sexes, now recognised in principle, should rapidly become a fact. That implies the promotion of women's participation in every field of civic life. In this respect the Council of Europe can play a role as stimulus and co-ordinator.

The Commission recommends in particular:

— implementation of an education policy for young people and adults aimed at affirming equality between the sexes as a value and at eradicating sexist stereotypes and preconceived ideas, and also at providing specific information and training for women in fields affecting every aspect of civic and political life;

— consideration of appropriate measures regarding working life in the public and private sectors intended to encourage and increase, from the stage of education and training onwards, women's presence in all sectors and at all levels;

— promotion of a code of conduct for the media, to ensure respect for women's dignity by advertisers and in the press.

CULTURE

Cultural identity

At the root of the European identity, throughout Europe's history, lies European culture, with its unity in diversity, based on freedom of the spirit and respect for mankind. Its manifold artistic, literary and scientific achievements are the common heritage of the peoples of Europe, which it is absolutely necessary to safeguard, enrich and develop without pause. While constituting a treasure of universal dimensions and an invaluable legacy to future generations, European culture must be enabled to extend its influence and its benefits to all parts of society without exception. Believing that the success of this mission depends very greatly on the Council of Europe's firm resolve to undertake effective joint action with its partners, the Commission recommends, in the spirit of the Stuttgart Declaration:[1]

a. Speedy fulfilment of all the conditions necessary for the proper working of the European Foundation in co-operation with the Council of Europe. To this end the Commission wishes to see the Foundation co-operate closely with a European Cultural Board, and recommends that the Council of Europe establish such a board to comprise independent figures, in particular creative and performing artists, scientists and academics, whose function would be to stimulate, guide and co-ordinate the development of European cultural co-operation;

b. Regular consultation between the Council of Europe and the European Community, to adopt and carry out specific projects on the lines of European Music Year 1985. Such projects should aim in particular:

— to train young people in the European spirit and in accordance with European values;

---

1. In the Solemn Declaration on European Union, adopted at Stuttgart on 19 June 1983, the Heads of State or Government of the member states of the European Community, meeting within the European Council, agreed to promote certain forms of action in the field of cultural co-operation "with a view to complementing Community action and stressing that, in consideration of the membership of their states in the Council of Europe, they maintain their firm support for and involvement in its cultural activities".

— to promote mutual understanding of each other's cultural preoccupations and production;

— to make Europeans aware of the universal significance of their civilisation by highlighting the multi-cultural dimension of European society;

— to aid all forms of creative activity by taking action to increase the material resources available for culture, including setting up a European Arts Fund and making taxation arrangements to increase private patronage and encourage private initiatives in any form.

Education and training of the young

A society which cuts itself off from its young people is a society in grave danger. Nowadays, the opportunities available to young people in terms of education, training, communication, travel, discoveries, culture, leisure, etc., go far beyond those available to previous generations. However, many young people are dissatisfied, frustrated and distressed as well as full of doubts about their future. It is true that the more educated, trained, informed and outward-looking young people are, the more aware they are of the shortcomings, defects and weaknesses of our societies, such as unemployment, social injustice, hunger and underdevelopment.

Considering that society's future lies with young people, the Commission took the view that one of its main tasks should be to offer some contribution to meeting their expectations.

The Commission considers that more should be done to involve young people in community life by encouraging their participation in decisions affecting them whether at local, national or European level. In this connection the Commission would like the efficacy of the European Youth Centre and the European Youth Foundation, institutions jointly managed by governments and European youth movements, to be enhanced.

The Commission considers that young people have a right to training. It believes that the education and training of the young still lack a true European dimension, without which the European identity and European mutual understanding cannot properly be affirmed. It therefore recommends:

— development of mobility among students, young people undergoing vocational training and teachers;

— recognition throughout Europe of certificates and qualifications;

— mobilisation of Europe's entire resources for the benefit of young people, in particular university networks and public and private cultural foundations;

— better foreign language learning;

— the introduction of a European dimension in all levels of education;

— fuller inter-university co-operation at European level.

Finally, the Commission believes that a European charter for students and young trainees should be drawn up with the participation of all interested parties, possibly incorporating the following:

i. Recognition of degrees, diplomas and studies:

— recognition in all Council of Europe member states of degrees and diplomas awarded or qualifications obtained in another European state;

— adoption of a European system of academic credits valid in all Council of Europe member countries;[1]

— European co-operation between universities with a view to setting up a University of Europe, composed of networks of existing university departments, to award a universally recognised European doctorate.

ii. A European dimension in education:

— improvement of modern language teaching at all levels;

— a more European approach to teaching, particularly of history, geography and literature, by such means as:

• promotion of exchanges of classes and teachers,

• creation in the universities of European chairs to provide opportunities for foreign teachers to pay short or extended visits to foreign universities;

— promotion of study and research visits abroad as part of the university curriculum, especially for the purpose of post-graduate diplomas;

— the setting up of a European Teachers' Centre to provide teachers with European training;

— promotion of a truly European civic education;

— celebration in schools of Europe Day on the same date in all countries of democratic Europe.

---

1. As proposed for the Community in the Adonnino report.

RESEARCH, SCIENCE AND TECHNOLOGY

The Commission observes that the sum total of national investment in research by European states is equivalent to investment in this field by other great powers, whether political or industrial, but that the results are not comparable, except in certain sectors. Being aware that progress in scientific and technical research is crucial to the future of European society, the Commission recommends mobilising Europe's potential, in the spirit of the resolutions of the Conference of European Ministers responsible for Research (Paris, 17 September 1984), by the following means:

— European co-ordination of national research programmes;

— development of networks for scientific and technical co-operation in Europe;

— closer association of other European states with Community research programmes.

In this connection the Commission welcomes the progress achieved by the Community following the Milan and Luxembourg European Councils towards more dynamic scientific co-operation in Europe. It also supports the Eureka project, and especially appreciates the fact that it is open to all European states interested.

The Commission believes, finally, that research in the social and human sciences should advance concurrently with scientific and technical research.

HARMONISATION OF LAW

The harmonisation of law, with which the Council of Europe and the European Community are alike concerned, is both a means and an end in progressing towards European unification. The effectiveness of the hundred or so European conventions negotiated in the Council of Europe is diminished by the large number of reservations and failures to ratify them.

The Commission recommends:

a. continuation of the work on harmonisation of law, in particular by the conclusion of conventions meeting the needs of the building of Europe;

b. a better follow-up of the conventions adopted, with a view to making them fully effective or, where necessary, revising them;

c. systematic accession by the Community to those conventions which concern matters within its competence;

d. a case-by-case investigation of the possibility of extending the standards adopted in the European Community to all Council of Europe member states.

REGIONAL AND LOCAL AUTHORITIES

The tendency towards decentralisation is very widespread in Europe; the European institutions should be better adapted to the preoccupations and expectations of local and regional authorities. To that end the Commission recommends:

a. that national delegations to the Council of Europe's Standing Conference of Local and Regional Authorities of Europe (CLRAE) be fully representative, at this European level, of the members of elected local and regional assemblies;

b. that the CLRAE or its national delegations be consulted by the Community institutions;

c. that the European Outline Convention on Transfrontier Co-operation between Territorial Communities or Authorities be ratified by all the Council of Europe member states concerned and that pilot transfrontier co-operation projects be carried out;

d. that the possibility be investigated of extending to all frontiers between Council of Europe member states, on the basis of reciprocity, the facilities for free movement of persons at the Community's internal frontiers.

MEANS OF CO-OPERATION

The Commission considers that co-operation between European democratic states differs in nature from traditional international co-operation and will progress only if the relevant institutions have appropriate resources. It consequently recommends:

a. that national budgetary contributions to organisations for co-operation between European democratic states (first and foremost the Council of Europe) be kept distinct from contributions to other international organisations;

b. that conferences of specialist ministers, being authorities for promoting and implementing intergovernmental co-operation in their own fields of competence, be integrated into the institutional framework of the Council of Europe, subject to the co-ordinating function of the Committee of Ministers;

c. that efforts to create a unified European civil service be continued.

CONCLUSION

With the presentation of this report to the statutory organs of the Council of Europe, the Commission feels it has discharged the terms of reference it received under Assembly Recommendation 994 (1984).

The purpose of the Commission's recommendations is to suggest ways and means whereby Europe may advance step by step towards closer unity among Europeans, as envisaged both in the Statute of the Council of Europe and in the Treaty of Rome. The Council of Europe has a vital part to play in that process.

SALES AGENTS FOR PUBLICATIONS OF THE COUNCIL OF EUROPE

AUSTRALIA
Hunter Publications
58A, Gipps Street
AUS-3066 COLLINGWOOD, Victoria

AUSTRIA
Gerold und Co.
Graben 31
A-1011 VIENNA 1

BELGIUM
La Librairie européenne S.A.
244, rue de la Loi
B-1040 BRUSSELS

CYPRUS
MAM
The House of the Cyprus Book
P.O. Box 1722
CY-NICOSIA

DENMARK
Munksgaard Export and
Subscription Service
35, Nørre Søgade
DK-1370 COPENHAGEN K

FEDERAL REPUBLIC OF GERMANY
Verlag Dr. Hans Heger
Herderstrasse 56
Postfach 20 08 21
D-5300 BONN 2

GREECE
Librairie Kauffmann
28, rue Stadiou
GR-ATHENS 132

ICELAND
Snaebjörn Jonsson & Co. A.F.
The English Bookshop
Hafnarstroeti 9
IS-REYKJAVIK 101

IRELAND
Government Stationery Office
Publications Section
Bishop Street
IRL-DUBLIN 8

ITALY
Libreria Commissionaria Sansoni
Via Lamarmora 45
Casella Postale 552
I-FLORENCE 50121

NEW ZEALAND
Government Printing Office
Mulgrave Street
(Private Bag)
NZ-WELLINGTON

PAKISTAN
Tayyab M.S. Commercial Services
P.O. Box 16006
A-2/3, Usman Ghani Road
Manzoor Colony
PAK-KARACHI-44

PORTUGAL
Livraria Portugal
Rua do Carmo, 70
P-1200 LISBON

SPAIN
Mundi-Prensa Libros S.A.
Castelló 37
E-MADRID 1

SWEDEN
Aktiebolaget C. E. Fritzes
Regeringsgatan 12
Box 163 56
S-10327 STOCKHOLM

SWITZERLAND
Buchhandlung Heinimann & Co.
Kirchgasse 17
CH-8001 ZÜRICH

Librairie Payot
6, rue Grenus
CH-1211 GENEVA 11

TURKEY
Librairie Haset Kitapevi A.S.
469, Istiklâl Caddesi
Beyoglu
TR-ISTANBUL

UNITED KINGDOM
H.M. Stationery Office
Agency Section
51 Nine Elms Lane
GB-LONDON SW8 5DR

UNITED STATES and CANADA
Manhattan Publishing Company
80 Brook St., P.O. Box 650
CROTON, N.Y. 10520

STRASBOURG
Librairie Berger-Levrault
23, Place Broglie
F-67081 STRASBOURG Cedex